curious about

NIKE

BY RACHEL GRACK

AMICUS LEARNING

What are you

curious about?

Curious About is published by
Amicus Learning, an imprint of Amicus
P.O. Box 227, Mankato, MN 56002
www.amicuspublishing.us

Editor: Ana Brauer
Series Designer: Kathleen Petelinsek
Book Designer and Photo Researcher: Sara Hood

Library of Congress Cataloging-in-Publication Data
Names: Koestler-Grack, Rachel A., 1973– author.
Title: Curious about Nike / by Rachel Grack.
Description: Mankato, MN : Amicus Learning, an imprint of Amicus, [2026] | Series: Curious about favorite brands | Includes bibliographical references and index. | Audience term: Children | Audience: Ages 6–9 | Audience: Grades 2–3 | Summary: "Who invented Nike? Spark elementary readers' curiosity about the popular sports brand's history, products, and cultural impact with insightful questions and well-researched answers. Includes table of contents, glossary, further resources, and index"—Provided by publisher.
Identifiers: LCCN 2024050040 (print) | LCCN 2024050041 (ebook) | ISBN 9798892005135 (library binding) | ISBN 9798892005678 (paperback) | ISBN 9798892006217 (ebook)
Subjects: LCSH: Nike (Firm)—Juvenile literature. | Sport clothes industry—Juvenile literature. | Athletic shoes—Juvenile literature. | Brand name products—Juvenile literature.
Classification: LCC HD9948.5.U64 N55475 2026 (print) | LCC HD9948.5.U64 (ebook) | DDC 646.4/—dc23/eng/20241211
LC record available at https://lccn.loc.gov/2024050040
LC ebook record available at https://lccn.loc.gov/2024050041

Photo Credits: Alamy Stock Photo/Ascannio, 2, 8, frantic, 14–15, News Images LTD, 9, Richard Wayman, 5; Dreamstime/Bonniecocos, cover, 1; Getty Images/Christian Petersen, 18–19, Cindy Ord, 4, John Iacono, 2, 17, Kirby Lee, 3, 20–21; Pexels/Andrius Šimkus, 13, Kaone Makoko, 11; Newscom/Anthony Behar/Sipa USA, 6–7; Shutterstock/artyaroslav, 9, IMAD_2442, 9, Lottie Lubbock, 9, Nattawit Khomsanit, 9; The Noun Project/Idwan Kurnia, 22, Maxicons, 22, Md Moniruzzaman, 23; Wikimedia Commons/Carolyn Davidson, 12, Carolyn Davidson, Nike, 12, 23, Nike, Inc., 12, unknown, 12

Printed in India

CHAPTER ONE

When did Nike start?

Nike's first pair of shoes came out in 1972.

In 1964. Phil Knight and Bill Bowerman opened Blue Ribbon Sports. They sold running shoes from Japan. In 1971, they started making their own styles. They renamed the company Nike. Today, Nike sells much more than shoes. It is the largest sports **brand** in the world.

Nike sells shoes for most sports.

DID YOU KNOW?
Nike is named after the Greek goddess of victory.

What was the first Nike shoe?

The Waffle Trainers quickly became a bestseller.

That would be Waffle Trainers. Bowerman wanted to make a shoe with a good grip. His breakfast gave him an idea: a waffle-shaped **tread**! He used his waffle iron to make the **sole**. The shoes dug into both dirt and grass. Nike still makes them.

DID YOU KNOW?

Waffle Trainers got the nickname "Moon Shoes." The bottoms reminded people of shoe prints on the Moon.

CHAPTER TWO

2

What is Nike's bestselling product?

Nike sells more than 780 million pairs of shoes each year.

Shoes, of course! Bowerman and Knight sold their running shoes at track meets. Soon, they started making footwear for other sports. They worked with athletes to build the best shoes. Nike became known for high **quality** and **performance**.

RUNNING
BASKETBALL
SOCCER
SKATEBOARDING
GOLF

When did Nike start making clothes?

In 1979, the company added the Windrunner. It was a lightweight jacket for runners. It was so stylish, people started wearing Nike for everyday use. The jacket became one of Nike's hottest sellers. It was a total game changer for the business.

Since 1979, Nike has made lots of clothing options.

What is "the swoosh"?

It is Nike's **logo**. A swoosh is the sound of movement, like a runner taking off. The saying "Just Do It" adds a push. It means quit thinking so hard and take that first step toward the finish line. You can be great. Afraid to try? Just do it.

NIKE LOGOS OVER THE YEARS

1964–1971

BLUE RIBBON SPORTS

1971–1978

1978–1985

1995–Present

Running shoes are one of Nike's most popular products.

Does Nike own any other companies?

Converse were made as basketball shoes in 1917.

Yes! Nike buys companies to build its product line. It bought Converse in 2003. Nike also owns the Air Jordan brand. Sometimes, Nike will sell a company after buying it. Products may come and go. These things often become collector's items.

When were Air Jordans made?

The first pair came out in April 1985. Michael Jordan signed a deal with the company when he was a **rookie**. Nike made a killer draft pick. Jordan became a basketball superstar. He is now the most famous face of Nike. There have been 38 lines of Air Jordans so far. They are an all-time bestseller.

Michael Jordan wore Air Jordans for the first time in November 1984.

CHAPTER THREE

Did the NBA ban Nike shoes?

Sort of. It once banned Air Jordans. In the National Basketball Association (NBA), basketball shoes were supposed to be mostly white or black. Jordan's black-and-red shoes broke the rules. He wore them anyway. The fine was $5,000 each game. Nike gladly paid it for him.

In 2024, Nike made a shoe line with Phoenix Suns player Devin Booker.

DID YOU KNOW?
The NBA changed its shoe rules in 2018. Players can now wear any color of shoe they like.

Can Nike shoes help you run faster?

Not really. But some shoes have a high **energy return**. They do not give you power. They just have a special sole. They put a spring in your step, and you lose less energy as you run. Nike's newest styles also use less energy to make. You may not run faster. But you help the environment. Swoosh!

Nike makes new shoes and clothes every year.

ASK MORE QUESTIONS

Which shoe is best for me?

What athletes have deals with Nike?

Try a BIG QUESTION: What type of sportswear would I design?

SEARCH FOR ANSWERS

Search the library catalog or the Internet.
A librarian, teacher, or parent can help you.

Using Keywords
Find the looking glass.

Keywords are the most important words in your question.

?

If you want to know about:

- shoes to try out, type: NIKE TRY BEFORE YOU BUY
- Nike deals, type: NIKE CELEBRITY ENDORSEMENTS

FIND GOOD SOURCES

Here are some good, safe sources you can use in your research.
Your librarian can help you find more.

Books

Nike
by Kenny Abdo, 2022.

Nike
by Sara Green, 2024.

Internet Sites

Kiddle: Nike, Inc. Facts for Kids
https://kids.kiddle.co/Nike,_Inc.
Kiddle is an online encyclopedia for kids.

Nike: Getting Kids Active
https://about.nike.com/en/impact/initiatives/getting-kids-active
Find out how Nike works to help kids stay active and healthy.

Every effort has been made to ensure that these websites are appropriate for children. However, because of the nature of the Internet, it is impossible to guarantee that these sites will remain active indefinitely or that their contents will not be altered.

SHARE AND TAKE ACTION

Design a new Nike shoe for any sport.

Run in different types of shoes.
Which shoes give you the best performance?

Talk about shoes with a friend.
What do you like about your favorite shoes?

GLOSSARY

brand A group of products made or owned by the same company.

energy return The amount of bounce inside the shoe after your foot lands on the ground.

logo A picture that stands for a company.

performance The action of carrying out an action, task, or function.

quality How well something is made.

rookie The first year an athlete plays a professional sport.

sole The outer bottom of a shoe.

tread The patterned surface on the bottom of a shoe.

INDEX

About the Author

Rachel Grack has been editing and writing children's books since 1999. She lives on a small ranch in southern Arizona. As a lover of stories, Disney is close to her heart. She also enjoys watching her grandchildren play Pokémon games on her Nintendo 64 console.